STORM CLOUDS ARE PASSING

Hold on Until Change Comes

Nikki Henderson

Foreword by

Joy Fields

authorHOUSE®

AuthorHouse™
1663 Liberty Drive
Bloomington, IN 47403
www.authorhouse.com
Phone: 1 (800) 839-8640

Published by AuthorHouse 07/20/2017

ISBN: 978-1-5246-9998-7 (sc)
ISBN: 978-1-5246-9997-0 (hc)
ISBN: 978-1-5462-0014-7 (e)

Library of Congress Control Number: 2017910969

Print information available on the last page.

Scripture quotations marked NLT are taken from the Holy Bible, New Living Translation, copyright © 1996, 2004, 2007. Used by permission of Tyndale House Publishers, Inc. Carol Stream, Illinois 60188. All rights reserved. Website

Any people depicted in stock imagery provided by Thinkstock are models, and such images are being used for illustrative purposes only. Certain stock imagery © Thinkstock.

This book is printed on acid-free paper.

CONTENTS

Dedication vii

Acknowledgements... ix

Foreword... xi

Introduction...xvii

Chapter One   Creation of the Storm 1

Chapter Two: Qualification for the Storm 7

Chapter Three: Decision Making when the Storm Arrives 13

Chapter Four: The Arrival of the Storm 20

Chapter Five: Worshipping Thru the Storm................................ 28

Chapter Six: Loving Yourself and Others Thru the Storm........ 38

Chapter Seven: Growing Thru the Storm 44

Chapter Eight: You've Sighed Long Enough – It's time for
                   you to cry out! 51

Chapter Nine: Be Careful who you Listen to During the Storm .. 58

Chapter Ten: Your Response is Critical During the Storm 65

Chapter Eleven: Forgiveness During and After the Storm.............. 72

Chapter Twelve: Rest Assure the Storm Will Pass 82

About the Author.. 87

DEDICATION

*This book is dedicated to my loving mother, Pauline and
my amazing father Norris, who have faithfully stood
beside me through every storm... unconditionally.*

ACKNOWLEDGEMENTS

To God – I have to say thank you for keeping me through it all. Truly I can tell the world that YOU ARE REAL. Thank you for giving me another chance to share with your precious people who will pick up this book. Thank you for loving me and bringing forth purpose in my life.

To My Mother – You have been such a strength to me that words can't even express. You have spoken words of life to me in the low times reminding me of who I was. Your strength for me and my sisters has made us the strong women that we are. Your prayers have shifted the atmosphere in so many lives. You are amazing. I love you Mom!

To My Father – Dad you are my own personal Superman! You have given so much over the years and have faithfully come to spend time with me and help me with my boys. I can call you day and night and you always answer. I love you Dad!

To My Other Mom – Willa you have stepped in to be a mom to me and I thank you. Thank you for the times we talk for hours and you listen and give me such sound advice. I love you!

To My Sons – Joshua and Jeremiah you are my hand-delivered miracles from God. Everything that I do is for you boys. I'm so humbled to be your mom and I cherish every moment we have. You are so blessed and favored by God and you are called to greatness. Thank you for going to bed on time so Mommy could write this book at night after long days at work (smile). I love you both so much!

To My Sisters – You both personally know the many storms I faced which could not even be written on these pages. You both have been a loving support. Tai – you are younger than me but always functioned as my big sister (smile). Your old soul and compassion allows you to help others thru their storms even as you endure your own. Your strength is indescribable. Kima – You have weathered storms that others could not survive. You are our miracle and I thank you for who you have been in my life.

To Rev. Lloyd Reid & First Lady Reid – Truly I am able to write this book because of you both and your amazing leadership. You both saw the small ember of light that was still there even in the midst of the storm. My soul has been nurtured back to health under your leadership at Greater Mount Bethel (Bronx, NY) over these past few years. I am eternally grateful to you both.

To My Greater Mount Bethel (GMB) Family – Every person should have a place to go where they feel safe and loved. And truly GMB has been that place for me since I was a little girl. To our Mothers of the Church who prayed me thru as a teenager and then as a grown woman, I say thank you. I cherish all of my GMB family and I thank you for your love and support for me and my family.

To Rev. Joy Fields – When I asked you to write the foreword, you didn't hesitate. And truly every word was written from the heart of a woman who truly knows me. From the time I met you over 20 years ago until now – I admire the amazing woman that you are. You are an inspiration to everyone that you encounter. Thank you for being my friend and believing in me.

To all My Friends and Family - There are so many to name and acknowledge. It would require me to write a whole book just for acknowledgements. You all know who you are. Your consistent, unconditional love and support has allowed me to get here. Thank you and I love you!

Lastly to My Storms – I didn't welcome you when you arrived but I now realize that you only passed thru to make me stronger. I am a Survivor! Because of my storms, I can encourage someone else and remind them that the STORM CLOUDS WILL PASS.

FOREWORD

A woman for all seasons—that's who you want with you when you encounter the storms of life. Nikki Henderson is a woman who has faced turbulent weather and shed many tears, but has maintained her strength through the joy of the Lord. Nikki ventures to train all of us to go through our storms successfully and come out fully qualified to walk into our new season.

When Nikki and I met over twenty years ago, she was a sweet spirit with a heart for God and a powerful worship. As the oldest child, she strove to bear some of the load for her struggling, single-parent mother and to consistently support her younger sisters. It was during her mother's storms that Nikki developed her own motherly sensibilities—the nurturing, the dreaming, the empowering, the praying and the pressing. She learned how to focus her energies on helping others successfully face their own situations and transform their dreams into reality. During this time, she also continued to make progress personally, spiritually and academically.

Nikki's storms intensified when she got married. Though she did what she knew to do to maintain a healthy marriage, pain from her past had built up walls and heart-wrenching experiences in her relationship lingered instead of passing by. The acute emotions, the staggering realities, the crumbling marriage often felt too much to bear. Yet in the midst of her storm, two miracle children were born. Nikki faced the angst of wondering if her premature newborns would thrive enough to leave the hospital and live beyond their first year. She knows what it is to watch her child turn blue and cold, life seeming to slip away. She knows the sleepless nights of watching, praying and crying, only to continue the cycle the next day. She's been in the position of facing tough decisions and hoping she made the right ones. Through it all, she has found the Lord to not only be faithful, but to be the One who sustained her mind, provided resources, gave her favor and taught her how to come out on the other side with a song of triumph.

At no point does Nikki present herself as a woman who has made all the right decisions, but rather as a woman who is willing to be honest about where she's been, how she got there, how the Lord navigated her through and what she gained in the process. As you journey through <u>Storm Clouds Are Passing</u>, expect to be fortified with internal strength to confront the storms of your life. Some storms pass quickly; others, linger, but no matter what kind of storm you face, this book will be like an anchor that keeps you from being swept away. If you receive the coaching from this storm warrior, you'll find Nikki's words will position you to embrace your life with the grace, joy, peace and prosperity God has always intended for you. God never promised life would be easy, but He promised He would be with you through it all.

Storm Clouds Are Passing is a thorough guide that will lead you step by step through the tumultuous situations that arise in life. It will prepare you for inevitable turbulence, teach you how to maintain composure in high pressure situations, show you techniques for thriving and encourage you to hold on during your storm. Imagine the relief you'll experience when this book helps you confront the feelings and thoughts you've had but never verbalized or acknowledged. There may be some "Ah ha!" moments as you learn the new ways this manual will teach you to perceive and embrace your storm. Wisdom, like precious gems, will be discovered and treasured as you learn to value the gift of the storm. Believe it or not, you may just end up thanking God for your storm when this book safely navigates you through to the other side.

So, I invite you to read and re-read Storm Clouds Are Passing. Ponder the reflection questions and search for the honest answers deep within your heart. Let Nikki's story prepare and inspire you to transform your storm from a terrifying experience seeking to destroy you to the terrific season that makes you whole.

Rev. Joy Fields

Author of Prom Passions: A Young Woman's Guide To Her Best Night Ever

Pastor, Century Church, South Plainfield, NJ

One day Jesus said to his disciples, "Let's cross to the other side of the lake." So they got into a boat and started out. As they sailed across, Jesus settled down for a nap. But soon a fierce storm came down on the lake. The boat was filling with water, and they were in real danger.

The disciples went and woke him up, shouting, "Master, Master, we're going to drown!" When Jesus woke up, he rebuked the wind and the raging waves. Suddenly the storm stopped and all was calm. Then he asked them, "Where is your faith?"

—Luke 8: 22 - 25

INTRODUCTION

While riding in the car with my sons on a Friday evening, they began to share with me the various names of the clouds in the sky. "It's a cumulus cloud Mommy, right over there", Jeremiah said excitedly. Joshua chimed in with his opinion stating, "It's a cirrus cloud over there Mommy". This went on for a couple of minutes. They didn't ask for my opinion. But I'm not sure if I had an opinion on the subject of the clouds. At that moment all I felt was storm clouds – unrealized hopes and dreams. I felt overwhelmed. My faith was wavering despite being a Christian for 21 years of my life. It was in that moment the words my Pastor spoke to me just a few days before resonated in my heart – "Storm Clouds are Passing".

What do you do when the storm has arrived? Weather can be unpredictable in the natural sense, and the same unpredictability exists in our lives at times. But the real question is not what you will look like when the storm arrives, but rather what will you look like when the storm is over and has passed by. No matter what your circumstances are, there is a guarantee that the storm clouds will pass one day. You must simply hold on.

As I sat down at my kitchen table to write one night, I asked God this question – "Who am I writing this book for?". And in that moment, I knew who it was for. It's for the person who has sat at their table with their hands on their head wondering what to do next. This book is for the man or woman who has wallowed in regret over choices made with no way to change them. This is for the one who has dealt with the pain of loss in their life – in one way or another. The one who is bound by guilt and shame because of their past. I'm writing to the single parent hoping to make ends meet. To the married couple who is almost at the end of their road.

Most importantly, there are some who will pick up this book and they are going thru the storm <u>right now</u>. And you picked up this book hoping to hear a word from God, a word of encouragement, a word of hope to remind you that the storm clouds are passing. God is sending a message to you today, right now, to let you know that the storm clouds may be here but they are passing by. You are on the brink of a shift in the season of your life. All you have to do is hold on just a little while longer. All you need is just a little more patience to ride out the storm. All you need is a small mustard seed of faith to move your mountain.

You are the one I'm writing this book for. I have suffered much from a little girl to this very day I write these words. I'm a witness that the storm clouds do pass. How you handle the time in between your hardship and your blessing is what counts. That is the predictor of what you will look like as the storm passes over. I pray that the words on these pages will be a blessing to you and build your faith as God inspires me to share from my heart to yours. We all have different journeys in this life. But we have one ability in common – the ability to hold on until your change comes. What is change? Change is a transformation of your situation in current state to the next phase of your existence.

My prayer is that as you journey through the words on the pages of this book, you will experience a transformation that will be evident in your life. At the end of every chapter will be thoughts to ponder and scriptures throughout the book to build your faith. I encourage you to grab a journal and spend time writing to reflect and record the still small voice that speaks even in the midst of the storm.

Chapter One

CREATION OF THE STORM

I wake up every morning and turn on the local news with the primary purpose of knowing the weather report for that day. There is one particular meteorologist I watch every day. I've grown used to his humor as he gives the weather update and I can sense his urgency when there is a change in the weather pattern. Living in New Jersey provides the opportunity to experience all types of weather patterns throughout the year. There's no doubt that the weather report is a vital part of my day. I am able to dress appropriately for whatever lies ahead. Have you ever noticed someone with a pair of shorts on when you know the forecast was the very opposite?

You wonder if they got the memo about what lies ahead. Or if they received the memo of the weather ahead – but chose to ignore it and dress for another season.

Merriam Webster defines meteorology as the atmospheric phenomena and weather of a region. In a broad physical sense, the atmosphere is the whole mass of air surrounding the Earth. However, the atmosphere can also be related to the air of a locality. Have you ever had the experience where you are driving in rain and suddenly it stops and the road you are on shows no evidence of rain prior? It's almost as if that rain cloud hovered over one particular area and when you drive out of it, you are suddenly back in the sunshine! I've always found that fascinating.

If we look at the concept of an atmosphere as a surrounding influence or environment then it can explain the reasoning on why I may be experiencing a storm cloud while my neighbor just a few blocks away may not have a storm at all. But the amazing part about an atmosphere is that is not stagnant. Even the worst storms in United States history had to move on when the storm was complete. The very nature of an atmosphere and weather is there is always movement. With this being said, there is hope that the storms of life that you face will pass over.

There are storms in life which we get the weather report for in advance and we are aware it is on the way. We can prepare effectively for those storms by securing any outdoor furniture, boarding windows and doors, ensuring we have an umbrella and rain gear if needed. These storms may seem easier to deal with because you can anticipate the outcome. Back in 2012, one of the worst storms hit the East Coast by the name of Hurricane Sandy. I can recall watching the storm hit New Jersey and losing power for days. The gas station lines were long, and banks were closed. If you didn't prepare with candles or generators ahead of time, you were guaranteed to be in the dark for days to come. That was a storm where the report of it coming was clear, but getting through the storm was the key.

I experienced a significant storm when I had my first child prematurely at 27 weeks, it was extremely difficult to deal with everything. His little 2 pound body seemed so frail with all the tubes hanging off of him. I didn't understand the Neonatal Intensive Care Unit and the processes involved in making my baby well. Whenever there were setbacks in his condition it felt like daily storms and it was devastating. As time went on I learned about high risk pregnancies and prematurity. So when I became pregnant with my second child, my doctors anticipated the storm ahead and began to prepare early. I had weekly progesterone injections and I was placed on bedrest very early. I saw my doctor every week and had more ultrasounds than I could count. When my second son arrived at 30 weeks, I was able to anticipate the process because I had -learned through my first storm.

A storm will never be worth it unless you learn while you are in the middle of it. The human tendency is to feel sorry for ourselves and question why we even have to go through the pain and struggle. And in the middle of all of it we miss those silent lessons that come to make us stronger. People around you that watch you go through the storm are more likely to remember what you looked like after the storm rather than what you looked like before. I've seen friends from the past and have been able to say "Wow, after all he or she has been through look how great they look". But if we don't grab hold of the lessons in the storm then we will miss the glory that comes after the story.

When I think back on my life, I realize that there were situations in my early years that may have caused the storm to brew. I was born in Landstuhl, Germany to two young soldiers – one from Alabama and one from Jamaica, West Indies. Two very different people from different cultures experience a connection of their worlds in the U.S. Army. While I can't remember many of those days, I can recall my mother reminding me that I spoke German fluently as a baby. Can you imagine! But all the while the storm of divorce and separation was brewing – threatening to destroy the comfort zone created by God. By the time I was 5 years old, I can recall moving to New York City with my mother and meeting my grandmother in New York for the first time. Many nights I listened to my mother cry as she struggled through the calamity of divorce and separation. She would close her door, and pray. Most of her prayers not words, but tears.

Day and night I have only tears for food, while my enemies continually taunt me, saying, "Where is this God of yours?" Psalms 42:3 (NLT)

As a little girl, never would I have imagined that I too would close my doors and weep in the same storm as my mother. There are cycles that ravage families and cause the storms to create and linger. But we must make a decision to change the atmosphere as soon as the storm is over to cause it not to brew in that same way again. If God has delivered you, don't be the victim any longer but become the victor! Tell that storm that you made it and the atmosphere has changed and been released. The arrival and passing of a storm means there was a shift in the atmosphere. While you are in the storm, you must speak to the atmosphere in your life and pray for the shift to occur. There is no storm that you are in that God is not there.

3 Thoughts to Ponder:

An atmosphere is not stagnant – a storm cloud must move on.

A storm will never be worth it unless you learn while you are in the middle of it.

While you are in the storm, you must speak to the atmosphere in your life and pray for the shift to occur.

Journal Moments:

1. What significant event has taken place in your life that you would classify as a storm?
2. If you were informed of a storm on the way, how would you prepare (naturally and spiritually)?

3. Are there are difficult times in your life that came about due to decisions you made? If so, what were the lessons you think you were meant to learn from it?

Take time on the next few pages to record your thoughts

1. What significant event has taken place in your life that you would classify as a storm?

_____

_____

_____

_____

_____

_____

_____

_____

_____

_____

_____

_____

_____

_____

_____

2. If you were informed of a storm on the way, how would you prepare (naturally and spiritually)?

_____

_____

_____

_____

_____

_____

_____
_____
_____
_____
_____
_____
_____
_____
_____
_____
_____

3. Are there are difficult times in your life that came about due to decisions you made? If so, what were the lessons you think you were meant to learn from it?

_____
_____
_____
_____
_____
_____
_____
_____
_____
_____
_____
_____
_____
_____
_____
_____

Chapter Two

QUALIFICATION
FOR THE STORM

Throughout this book, I will make reference to the biblical account of a man named Job.

Job was a wealthy and religious man who appeared to have life under control. Job 1:1 -5 describes Job in this way:

> *There once was a man named Job who lived in the land of Uz. He was blameless – a man of complete integrity. He feared God and stayed away from evil. He had seven sons and three daughters. He owned 7,000 sheep, 3,000 camels, 500 teams of oxen, and 500 female donkeys. He also had many servants. He was, in fact, the richest person in the entire area. Job's sons would take turns preparing feasts in their homes, and they would also invite their three sisters to celebrate with them. When these celebrations ended – sometimes after several days – Job would purify his children. He would get up early in the morning and offer a burnt offering for each of them. For Job said to himself, "Perhaps my children have sinned and have cursed God in their hearts". This was Job's regular practice.*

In modern day perception, Job "had it all together". I imagine he was a good husband and father, great credit, wealthy and healthy. I'm sure every day of his life was not a walk in the park, but generally he would have no worries. He shunned evil which indicates he had a no nonsense attitude for what was not right in the sight of God. He would even make arrangements for the purification of his children because he was concerned about their souls and their relationship with God. He was the greatest man among all the people of the east.

You may be thinking "I don't fit that picture" and "That's not my life story!". Many of us are living with bad decisions that have taken our lives off course. We deal with lack and emotional poverty that holds us back from pursuing our dreams. Shame and guilt hold us captive to our past. When the storms show up it's easy to point the blame at someone else and even ourselves. We feel there is something we have done that must have qualified us for the storm.

Although I did my best to have a healthy pregnancy, my children were born prematurely. And many days as I walked the hospital corridor I tried to retrace my steps to see what qualified me for this storm. I read books on prematurity attempting to diagnose my own situation. All statistics and medical advice explained to me that there was no one specific reason for premature birth. Yet, I felt guilt and wanted to find the root of my storm.

Scientifically, thunderstorms are formed by the action of warm air rising and cold air sinking. Three of the most important ingredients for thunderstorm formation is unstable air, moisture, and lift. As I reflected on the thunderstorm formation elements, I realized that there were some times of instability in my life that brought on the storms. Maybe my judgement was not on point as I ventured into relationships. Possibly a bad financial deal was the element that caused a storm to brew. Moisture is a sign of water without the liquid flow of water. Are there parts of your life where you have a sign of something but not the full outflow? Too much moisture or too little moisture can be good or bad depending on what it comes in contact with. Moisture in a room can keep it humidified for clear breathing at a certain level, but too much moisture can cause mildew which is unsafe for breathing. You have to examine your life to determine if there are things or people in your life which are meant for a season but if they stay longer they can do damage, hence the formation of a storm. Lastly, a lift is needed in order to move the storm. This is evident because it is windy when a storm is on its way. You will notice the wind pick up and begin moving things around.

So how does Job fit in topic of storms? As you will see on our journey together, Job was a key candidate for the storm. See, the storms of life may not show up based on how good or bad you have been. The storms of life don't look for how much money is in your bank account. It is simply a weather pattern that comes through an atmosphere for an intended purpose. As you continue to read, my prayer is that you will see that like Job, the storm was never intended to kill you. Yes, it may very well feel as if you are dying. You may be struggling with depression and anxiety as everything goes wrong. But you must know that you are qualified for the storm.

One day the members of the heavenly court came to present themselves before the Lord, and the Accuser, Satan, came

> *with them. "Where have you come from?" the Lord asked Satan (Job 1:6 – 8). Satan answered the Lord, "I have been patrolling the earth, watching everything that's going on". Then the Lord asked Satan, "Have you noticed my servant Job? He is the finest man in all the earth. He is blameless – a man of complete integrity. He fears God and stays away from evil." (Job 6:1-8)*

This look into the heavenly transaction regarding Job's life was a clear indicator that God knew that Job was capable of handling the storm.

It may be difficult to embrace the fact that God allowed Job to be tested. There have been times in my life where I asked God "Why?". As I grew in my faith, and matured in the Word of God, I began to hold on to verses like Romans 8:28 which says "And we know that God causes everything to work together for the good of those who love God and are called according to his purpose for them". I could rest in knowing that the storm of hurt and pain was not meant to kill me, rather it would leave me as a survivor to help others. Today, I can pray with strong conviction. I was qualified for my storm.

3 Thoughts to Ponder:

When the storms show up it's easy to point the blame at someone else and even ourselves.

You have to examine your life to determine if there are things or people in your life which are meant for a season but if they stay longer they can do damage, hence the formation of a storm.

You must know that you are qualified for the storm.

Journal Moments:

1. Have you ever felt like Job – doing all the right things but still experiencing difficulty? How did you handle that?

2. What strengths did you see in yourself that you didn't know where there before your difficult season?

3. How can you turn your painful moments into helpful moments for others?

Take time on the next few pages to record your thoughts

1. Have you ever felt like Job – doing all the right things but still experiencing difficulty? How did you handle that?

_____
_____
_____
_____
_____
_____
_____
_____
_____
_____
_____
_____
_____
_____
_____
_____

2. What strengths did you see in yourself that you didn't know where there before your difficult season?

_____
_____
_____
_____
_____
_____

_____
_____
_____
_____
_____
_____
_____
_____
_____
_____

3. How can you turn your painful moments into helpful moments for others?

_____
_____
_____
_____
_____
_____
_____
_____
_____
_____
_____
_____
_____
_____
_____
_____
_____

Chapter Three

DECISION MAKING WHEN THE STORM ARRIVES

My youngest child learned about storms during his science curriculum at school and he became fascinated and afraid as well. When he realized that the concepts being taught by his teacher were not just in a book, but could also manifest in the natural it became troubling for him. One day we were out on our way to a restaurant for dinner and a storm showed up. He said "Turn back Mommy! Let's go back home!". He was literally in tears. I began to feel nervous driving through the storm but I was in a place of decision. Either I turn back home or keep going to the restaurant. When I calculated my current location, my destination was closer. While home appeared to be the safest place, it was more logical to press forward to the restaurant and seek shelter there.

<u>When the storm clouds are raging in your life – think before you act</u>. Stop for a moment and calculate where you are. You need to decide if it's worth turning back or pressing forward. Your finances may be in red, but is it worth you resorting to where you were before. Or do you continue to foster good habits, focus on your spending and saving so you can reach your destination? Your marriage may be under attack and everything is going wrong, but is it worth you filing for divorce or is there enough to hold on for just a little longer?

What is logical and safe is not always where God desires you to be. <u>Sometimes God allows the storm to arrive so you can make a decision</u>. The storm arrived, I was on the road already close to my destination. When I got there, we ran inside (and got soaked instantly by all the rain). The lights in the restaurant blinked on and off a few times threatening a power outage. But yet I felt safe knowing I was among others. By the time we had our meal, the storm was passing over. What will you do when the storm arrives? Even as you read this book I want you to take a moment and reflect on how you have reacted when storms arrived in your life. Did you run from the crisis? When the storm arrives, stop and calculate where you are. The logical decision may not be the right decision.

The Bible gives us these Words to Live By in Decision Making:

> *Trust in the Lord with all your heart; do not depend on your own understanding. Seek his will in all you do and he will show you which path to take (Proverbs 3:5-6).*

Don't worry about anything; instead pray about everything.
Tell God what you need, and thank him for all he has done.
Then you will experience God's peace, which exceeds anything
we can understand. His peace will guard your hearts and
minds as you live in Christ Jesus (Phillipians 4:6-7).

We can make our plans, but the Lord determines our steps
(Proverbs 16:9).

These are just a few scriptures. I admonish you to take the time to read scriptures in regards to decision making so your heart can be filled with direction. The unrest of a storm can cause you to make irrational decisions. The winds blow and you must be able to withstand the winds of the storm. My mother always tells me, "Nicole, don't make decisions while you are going through". You must make a decision to stand flat-footed in your storm. My mother became ill while pregnant with me. The daunting onset of bell palsy caused her to experience a stroke with the hurtful evidence of a misfigured face. Truly she was in a storm. Her mind must have wondered, "Why did I live to go through this physical shame?" But had she not held strong to her decision to live, I would not be writing this book today.

I know from experience that sometimes the first inclination is to run in a storm. Don't feel bad! It's apart of your natural make-up! It's called the Fight-or-Flight response. Fight-or-Flight response is a physiological reaction that occurs in humans in response to a perceived harmful event, attack, or threat to survival. The reaction begins in the brain and goes through a process of releasing the hormone cortisol which increases blood pressure, blood sugar, and suppresses the immune system. This sounds really complicated and stressful for the body. But the reality is some of us operate in this state constantly. We can hear a person's name and we immediately activate fight or flight! Our thoughts of constant worry and negativity can put us in this state from the time we wake up and even during our sleep at night.

The purpose of the hormone release is to boost energy so we can react. Our heart accelerates, our lung action accelerates, and even our muscles tense up to either fight or run. But here is the troubling part: we get our bodies into this state and we end up taking no action at all. You are frozen and stagnant. You can't make a decision to run or fight. You actually are going thru the motions of getting ready to take action… but never getting to the point of action. I can imagine my body screaming "Nikki, stop doing this to me! It's stressful!". Your body may just well be saying the same.

My sincere prayer is that you too will make the right decision in the storm. Your decision may be the simple element of just deciding to live through the storm you are facing in life. I pray against suicidal thoughts and nervous breakdowns right now in the name of Jesus! I intercede for your mind, body, and soul. In this moment, you shall make the decision to live!

Say this prayer:

> *Lord Jesus, I know you formed me from the dust of the earth. And you didn't stop there Lord. You breathed the breath of life into me (Genesis 2:7). I know I can live because you are the way and the truth, and the life. No one can come to the Father except through you (John 14:13). As I face my storms, help me to feel your love because no greater love than a man would lay down his life for a friend (John 15:13). I choose life and that more abundantly. I choose to live through the storm.*

That simple prayer is effective because you are declaring the Word of God over your life and your situation. The Word of God is powerful and sharper than any two edged sword! The decisions you make upon the arrival of the storm will determine your outcome. You may not know what decision to make right now, but take the time to pray and ask God for direction. <u>Every decision is a lasting decision. Regret is a robber of your mental energy.</u> Prayer in the midst of a storm is key because remember the storm clouds are passing. It won't be like this always. You will see the light of day. If you are reading this book and you have been thru a storm and come thru on the other side – you can attest to the fact that there is light at the end of the tunnel.

The light can be very dim at times. I truly didn't see the light at the end of my tunnel. When my youngest son was born with hemorrhaging on the brain, the anxiety of cerebal palsy being his outcome was looming over my head. For 6 months, I stretched his legs and arms and spoke to his mobility through the Power of God. I commanded his legs to stretch as they should. I prayed and cried because I was still dealing with the after effects of prematurity with my first son who was only 2 years old at the time. Two children, two bleak diagnosis, crumbling marriage equaled no light for me. But I kept praising, I kept crying out to God, even in the midst of my storm. I knew there was a day when I would wake up and say "It's ok". Those two small words coming from <u>your mouth</u> about <u>your situation</u> is one of the most powerful moments you will experience. Not because everything turned out perfect – but because you survived!

The most important decision you can make at this time is to Live. Just decide to live. The storm clouds are passing.

---

3 Thoughts to Ponder:

When the storms clouds are raging in your life—think before you act.

Sometimes God allows the storm to arrive so you can make a decision.

Regret is a robber of your mental energy.

Journal Moments:

1. Think about some major decisions you have made in a time of unrest. What was the outcome?
2. How often do you pray about the areas of concern in your life? Do you need to increase the time you take to pray? How can that benefit you?
3. Think about a great decision you have made recently. Record the decision and celebrate your accomplishment thru writing encouraging words to yourself.

Take time on the next few pages to record your thoughts

1. Think about some major decisions you have made in a time of unrest. What was the outcome?

_____
_____
_____
_____
_____
_____
_____
_____
_____
_____
_____
_____
_____
_____
_____
_____
_____
_____

2. How often do you pray about the areas of concern in your life? Do you need to increase the time you take to pray? How can that benefit you?

_____
_____
_____
_____
_____
_____
_____
_____
_____
_____
_____
_____
_____
_____
_____
_____

_____

_____

_____

3. Think about a great decision you have made recently. Record the decision and celebrate your accomplishment thru writing encouraging words to yourself.

Chapter Four

THE ARRIVAL
OF THE STORM

Job was going about a normal day at home while his children were feasting at his oldest son's house. Suddenly Job's storm arrived. In one day, four messengers came simultaneously to provide the news of the storm clouds looming over Job's life. Have you ever received bad news that seemed to rock your world? Maybe it was a doctor's report after just going in for a routine check-up with a diagnosis of diabetes, hypertension, or even cancer. Maybe it was a sudden death of a family member or friend that rendered you speechless. Whatever the extreme may be, hearing that something bad has occurred is heart-wrenching.

> *One day when Job's sons and daughters were feasting and drinking wine at the oldest brother's house, a messenger came to Job and said, "The oxen were plowing and the donkeys were grazing nearby, and the Sabeans attacked and made off with them. They put the servants to the sword, and I am the only one who has escaped to tell you!"*

Job 1: 13 – 15

Job receives message that his enemy has attacked his farmland and captured all his animals and put all the servants to the sword. There is just one messenger who escaped to tell the story. The oxen was a large beast that is believed to be the ancestor of the domestic cattle. It symbolized ferocious strength. Oxen were extremely valuable as a work animal. They were often yoked in pairs to do the farm work and were used to transport burdens. They were permitted as food and also offered as sacrifices. Donkeys were also valuable animals and used for riding by leaders. Owning a large number of donkeys was a sign of wealth.

The first area the storm hit was Job's finances. All his animals were stolen and he was without transportation or servants to work the land. In our current economic state, many of us face financial troubles and burdens. No matter what your race or gender, there is a chance that a financial storm can hit your life. Someone may have had a great job one day and laid off the next wondering how they will meet their expenses. I remember as a single mom after divorce, watching everything slip through my fingers. When I moved into my first apartment as a single woman again eight years ago, all I had was a mattress for me and my three-year old and a toddler bed for my one-year old. We had a light green couch chair that a friend gave me and I found a $40 television stand from a warehouse that sold second hand furniture along with a $28 television. For many nights I went home and slept on that uncomfortable bed. One of my mutual friends through a couple I knew was selling her home and gave me a call. She heard that I moved and needed some furniture and wanted to give me some items. I called a friend, rented a U-haul truck and came back home with a sofa and loveseat, beautiful kitchen plates and cups, a microwave and so many more things that I'm forever grateful to her for. You never know who God will send to bless you in the middle of your storm.

Sometimes the storm clouds come to humble and remind us of the grace and mercy of God. I went from being in a two-income household to a one income household. I had to learn how to balance out my money and make it work. There was a time when I went to the supermarket with $10 and could plan an entire week of meals. I learned how to budget and look for the best deals. But most of all I learned how to sacrifice for the sake of my children. One pair of black pumps was all I had to go to my job in corporate America. I sacrificed my own image so that I could ensure that we had a roof over our head, lights stayed on, food on the table and there was never a day of lack. The support I received from their father helped to balance out the childcare fees and all the other expenses that come from having small children. But there were days when it felt like it was never enough. But God was just building me up as I went through the storm. As I look back now I can see how I've grown in the management of finances and understanding debt. A credit card bill keeps me up a night! I've learned that the less I can owe, the more I can save. I'm focused on the goal of being debt free in and after the storm.

When things are going smoothly, there is a tendency to become complacent and dependent on "stuff". But when you experience rock bottom, you appreciate the top. Not long after moving, my awesome mom came and took me to buy a bedframe and mattresses for me and my sons. We got a new dining room table and our place was finally looking like a home! Things were looking up for us. I cried many nights wondering how I was going to make it. The finances were in red, the bills were due, and the money was short. But eight years later, I praise God that I never received an eviction notice and not one day of hunger came to me and my children. Trust God in the storm. Trust him to meet you right where you are!

4 Ways to Weather the Financial Storm

1. Make sound financial decisions – Think about what you want your life to look like after the storm. Don't make decisions based on the moment, make the decisions based on your long-term goals. If your desire is to transition from a renter to a homeowner, don't give up because of the storm. Save what you can and pay your bills on time. You will be setting the stage for your next level, in the midst of what you are going through.

2. Use credit wisely – Try to resist the urge to use credit to mask the storm. Expensive clothing or a nice car while you are in a financial storm, may only serve as a band-aid that won't pull off too easily! Live in the moment. It's ok if you can't make the purchase right now. Just set a goal and work towards it. Remember, it's your condition on the inside that matters in the storm, not your outward appearance.

3. Save as much as you can – Habukuk 2:2 declares "Write the vision and make it plain on tablets, that he may run who reads it". Write your savings plan. Create a budget and hold yourself too it. Don't worry if you have a setback, just keep pressing forward in your process. Cutback where you can through strategies like taking your own lunch to work. You will be surprised at how much you save over the course of the year. Remember, you have to say No at times because your neighbor may not be experiencing the same storm. You must operate based on the season you are in and God's direction for your life.

4. Be a good steward of your finances – The hardest time to give is when you are in a storm. However, that's when God stretches you the most to give. Sow financial seeds into ministry, family, and even random people. You will find that as you help to meet the needs of someone else, God will meet your needs. There is also a great feeling that comes from being able to help others.

The first messenger brought news of Job's wealth being stripped by his raids on his oxen and donkeys. Job Chapter 1 gives the account of four messengers coming with news of the arrival of a storm. You may be able to relate. Some people seem to experience cycles of storms over and over again. I think of the saying "If ain't one thing, it's another". Another saying I recall repeating often was "When it rains in pours". I don't even know who taught me these sayings to describe cycling storms. I probably heard other adults saying it before I even knew what trouble was.

I want to speak from my heart to your heart from the Heart of God, thru these pages. It was difficult for me to initially write this book, because I was going thru my stormy season. And when I would come up for air with a fresh revelation – I would add a sentence here and a paragraph there. I understand that the stormy seasons in your life can be exhausting. If you are in the midst of the storm, you can relate. If you are on the other side of the storm, I'm sure you can still relate for yourself or to someone else close to you. The storm can arrive and thrust you into tears. On the other hand, the storm can arrive and make you numb. Loss for words and feelings. The word arrive means to make an appearance. I like this meaning because it has the tone that just as something appears – it can also disappear. Your storm does not have to linger. You can see the breaking of day again. It's on the horizon! Look up and look out around you! Psalms 123:1 declares *"I lift up my eyes to you, O God, enthroned in heaven"*.

Take a moment to look at the cover of this book. Your storms seems raging but if you look up you will see the season shifting. Don't let the noise of the storm outweigh your ability to look up! Arrival does not mean permanent residence. It only means an appearance, that doesn't have to last as long as you think it will.

> ## <u>3 Thoughts to Ponder:</u>
>
> *You never know who God will send to bless you in the midst of your storm.*
>
> *When things are going smoothly, there is a tendency to become complacent and dependent on "stuff".*
>
> *Your storm does not have to linger. You can see the breaking of day again.*

Journal Moments:

1. It can be difficult to embrace why "bad things" seem to happen to "good people". Record any struggles or thoughts you have had with that in your personal beliefs. This relief of releasing the thoughts onto paper can be very therapeutic.
2. Outline some strategies you think will be effective in your life when a storm arrives to help you remain on track.
3. Write your own personal prayer of thankfulness for the struggles that arrived but you survived.

Take time on the next few pages to record your thoughts

1. It can be difficult to embrace why "bad things" seem to happen to "good people". Record any struggles or thoughts you have had with that in your personal beliefs. This relief of releasing the thoughts onto paper can be very therapeutic.

_____

_____

_____

_____

_____

_____

_____

_____

_____

_____

_____

_____

_____

_____

2. Outline some strategies that you think will be effective in your life
   when a storm arrives to help you remain on track.

_____

_____

_____

_____

_____

_____

_____

_____

_____

_____

_____

_____

_____

_____

3. Write your own personal prayer of thankfulness for the struggles
   that arrived but you survived.

_____

_____

_____

_____

_____

_____

_____

_____

_____

_____

_____

_____

_____

_____

Chapter Five

WORSHIPPING THRU THE STORM

When I read the story of Job for the first time, an overwhelming feeling of sadness came over me as I realized that Job lost so much instantly. Job 1:20 says "Job stood up and tore his robe in grief. Then he shaved his head and fell to the ground to worship". If I had to finish this sentence, I would say "and Job fell down to the ground and wallowed in sorrow", or "Job fell down to the ground and fainted from shock", or "Job fell down to the ground in grief". Surely that would be my reactions to the storms Job faced! But the key here is Job fell down to the ground and worshipped! How can you worship when your world is falling apart? But the enemy expected Job to do the very opposite. He expected Job to curse God , yet Job went back to the very core of his being by saying,

"I came naked from my mother's womb, and I will be naked when I leave. The Lord gave me what I had, and the Lord has taken it away. Praise the name of the Lord!" (Job 1:21).

I was so baffled the first time I read this (just as you probably are) because it goes beyond the human understanding to worship in the middle of your storm. But when you realize that you are only here by the grace and mercy of God, it breeds a humility that goes beyond human emotion. I learned from Job that I have to remain a worshipper regardless of what I am going through. Worship is the human response to the perceived presence of the divine, a presence which transcends normal human activity and is holy. In order for Job to fall down to worship, he had to perceive that God was still in the midst of what he was going through! How amazing is that!

So many times we wait on cues to get into worship. I have always attended a Pentecostal church which is characterized by visual acts of worship, spirited preaching, and we love to sing! But as I grew in Christ, I learned that not everyone that sang and worshipped did it because they were so happy. Sometimes people worshipped because it was what they were being convinced to do. They were broken and numb. Many times we just have to worship from the broken places. I have always loved to sing before the Lord in my own private time and even dance before him.

And there have been times when I have felt such a powerful anointing surround me as I worshipped from the broken places. Worship is your human response to an Omnipotent God to say "I perceive you are here right with me in my storm!".

When the storm arrives, it is so easy to stop praising. It's so easy to stop reading your Bible. And it's really easy to stop praying and get on the phone to tell someone else all your troubles. But it is in that time when the storm has arrived that you must fall to your knees in prayer and say:

> *"Naked I came out of the womb and naked I will return. God I am so dependent on you in this time. I need you. My human response is to run far away. My human response is to be angry. But instead I make a decision to worship! Let the tears fall Lord! I will lay prostrate before you until my mind lines up with my spirit to say, I trust you regardless of what I am going through.*

I guarantee you that as you begin to worship, you will begin to sense a shift in your thinking to line up with your spirit man. Even as I write these words, I can sense it! There is a miraculous release in your worship during the midst of the storm. No matter how much I go through, I have to lift my hands to the Lord. I have to sing a song of my own. My words from my heart to God's ears. In the end you feel better knowing that you were able to bear your soul to such a Holy God. This transcends culture, race, or gender. Worship is universal and shatters the back of the enemy. Because it is the opposite of what it seems I should do in that moment.

There were so many days where I felt so down and depressed as I faced the storms of my life. But what I learned was that when I couldn't worship for myself, I would find a worshipper to bring me in. As a young woman, I discovered a cassette tape of Pastor Sheryl Brady. She is such an awesome worshipper. I would listen to that tape over and over again and it would usher me right into the presence of God. Oh how I wish I could find that cassette tape now over 20 years later! Thank God for Youtube and all the technology we have now. The point is, if you can't pull your heart into worship, find some music that will usher you in if you have to. Or simply fall to your knees and just wait for the breakthrough. God sees you and he knows you by name. He is concerned about your worship in the midst of the storm!

Your reaction while the storm clouds are passing will determine your condition when the sun shines again. Have you ever openly or secretly blamed God for allowing bad things to happen in your life? If you have, you are not alone. The human nature is to blame someone when things happen that are not favorable. When we have an accident at home like something falling and breaking, my sons may have been playing nicely. But the moment the accident or mishap occurs, they are pointing the fingers to determine who is responsible. And not only that, they are usually upset, crying, and downright angry. And that's what happens to us as we go through the mishaps of life. There are times where instead of praying and falling to our knees, we get angry and we point the finger. Job was such an influential man and I'm sure he had friends and family he could run to instantly. So many times when I was supposed to fall to my knees in the storm, I picked up the phone. But the conversation only caused to me to fester further into my issues. It was only to fall deeper into the trap of self-pity. Now I'm not against having someone to talk to about what you are going through. My mother is my ultimate confidant so I understand the need for someone to share even your most hurtful issues with. But there are times when like Job, I have to just fall to my knees in worship and prayer.

You may be there right now – the burden is so heavy. And even talking to your closest friend may not be meeting the need. I challenge you to find a quiet place – right now if you can. Challenge your heart and mind to quiet down and fall to your knees. I say <u>fall to your knees</u> because when you fall, there is a loss of balance that puts you in a position you didn't plan to be in. There is a letting go that has to occur when you fall into a position. Gravity has to take over and help you land on your knees. You have fallen into so many other positions. Why not now fall to your knees? There is no pain from loss of a loved one, to sickness, to divorce, to loneliness that God is not able to understand and heal. He knows every fragmented piece of your broken heart.

Like Job, my greatest comfort has come in my ability to worship the Lord regardless of what I am going through. In the past seven years, I have been through various situations which would have been a recipe for a nervous breakdown. But I believe it's been the falling to my knees that kept me in the storm. Remember, <u>the storm clouds are passing</u>. Don't throw away all your hopes and dreams in the middle of the storm. Truly I could relate to David in the Bible when he prayed in Psalms 77 and said:

> *I cry out to God; yes I shout. Oh, that God would listen to me! When I was deep in trouble, I searched for the Lord. All night long I prayed, with hands lifted towards heaven, but my soul was not comforted. I think of God, and I moan, overwhelmed with longing for his help. You don't let me sleep. I am too distressed even to pray! I think of the good old days, long since ended, when my nights were filled with joyful songs. I search my soul and ponder the difference now. (Psalms 77: 1-6)*

Truly David was in the middle of a storm. And he was being honest to his feelings inside. But what I love about this Psalm is that his prayer and worship did not stop there. Psalms 77:10-12 declares:

> *"And I said, "This is my fate; the Most High has turned his hand against me." But then I recall all you have done, O Lord; I remember your wonderful deeds of long ago. They are constantly in my thoughts. I cannot stop thinking about your mighty works.*

<u>David was declaring that regardless how he felt in the middle of his storm, he was going to remember what God had already done before the storm arrived</u>! While David poured out his heart before God, he was conscious of the fact that the storm was just passing. He knew that God's faithfulness had not diminished because of the storm. Although he felt the pain of his circumstances, he felt the hope of God's faithfulness.

One day recently, I was on the road driving my two boys to summer camp. The summer was winding down and I was beginning to worry about how they would do in their new school. They were in the backseat complaining about their camp saying how boring it was and they needed to attend a new camp next year. The combination of my own anxiety coupled with their complaining was definitely starting my day off on the wrong foot! I started to feed into their feelings and bring my dissatisfaction in to. And then suddenly I just began to say "Thank you". I started to thank God that they were safe all summer in camp. Thanking God that no one came in with weapons to hurt all the precious children. Thanking God that he provided the money I needed to pay for the camp each week. Thanking God they had lunch everyday!

Soon after it became contagious and they began to thank God too! Instead of whining and saying "Why me?" I began to worship during the storm instead! And the moment I began to open my mouth (as hard as it felt), the thank you began to flow out of my lips. And by the time I dropped them off, I was getting out the car still saying thank you. Of course at that point, with their little friends standing outside, they became a little embarrassed as I lifted my hands in worship (smile). But it didn't matter who saw me, because with just one moment of worship, my mind was transformed for the day and the rest of the summer! That experience taught me that even in the low moments, like Job and even David, there is still a place instead where we can be grateful and worship despite the circumstances.

I challenge you to find that place in your heart where you can worship despite the storm. Worship for each person may be different. For some it may be lifting their hands and crying out with a loud voice. For others, it may be kneeling to the ground with silent tears and only a few words as Job. But whatever you do, find your path to worship. Remember, the storm clouds are passing. Things won't be this way all the time. And the reality is you may have to read this book during multiple storms. But never lose the ability to worship during the storm.

Job uttered the words – "Naked I came out of the womb, and naked I will return". Have you ever had all your clothes on, yet you felt stripped? I don't think Job was concerned about the physical nakedness, as much as he was concerned about the nakedness of possession. When we come out of the womb, we are just a spirit, soul, mind and body. Fresh into this world with nothing but our senses to help us learn and gather what is around us. As time wears on, we get dressed in this process called life. But ironically, at the end of the day we are still naked. Sometimes our circumstances can cause us to come to a state of nakedness.

One loss of income, and suddenly you are naked in your finances. Stripped to the minimum. Bills are due, but the money will not suffice. Credits cards are maxed out and there is nowhere else to borrow. In those times, you feel like Job – naked. One night of infidelity and your marriage is ruined and suddenly you are naked in your heart. Broken, confused. In those times, you feel like Job – naked. The annual routine visit turns into a cancer diagnosis and your life is turned upside down – suddenly. Naked, worried, and sick. So I sat, and asked Lord, why did Job say this in the midst of his storm? As I pondered this thought, a still small voice whispered "Job realized his dependency on Me".

It was then that the tears began to fall because I needed to be more like Job. I needed to depend on God in my naked season. When all seems to be gone. And I was guilty of just trying to diagnose the situation instead of giving it all to God. Job realized that he came into this world with nothing and then when he leaves this world, he will leave with nothing. He realized that just as God gave, God could take away. And that is where his ability to worship came in. It was a deep seated humility to realize that he was dependent on God. Oh how that blessed me!

Because I realized that I had to grow up in my faith. And I challenge you to grab hold of this and raise your dependency on God.

Recently I was going through a situation that was very difficult for me. My father was visiting with me as he has done faithfully for the past seven years to help me with my sons and provide a helping hand with school pick-ups, and even giving me a movie night out to myself. We were talking about my situation and normally I would have begun complaining and speaking negatively. But this one night I looked at my father and said "Dad, God is not going to give me more than I can bear. So if I'm going through this, it must mean that I can do it". I didn't realize in that moment, that I was shifting the atmosphere in my home! I was saying to the enemy, come what may , come what might – I'm getting through this! It all equals dependency.

Your ability to worship through the storm will be dependent on how much you trust God and realize that your life is in His hands. Will you just continue to complain to whoever will listen. Or will you open your mouth and speak life?

> *"The tongue can bring life or death; those who love to talk will reap the consequences. Proverbs 18:21*

In this next season, it's how you speak is what will determine how you come out after the storm. Change your language! You may have to learn another language in order to change your language. Learn the word of God and speak it!

<u>Thoughts to Ponder:</u>

Worship is the human response to the perceived presence of the divine, a presence which transcends normal human activity and is holy.

There is no pain from loss of a loved one, to sickness, to divorce, to loneliness that God is not able to understand and heal. He knows every fragmented piece of your broken heart.

Don't throw away all your hopes and dreams in the middle of the storm.

Journal Moments:

1. What does worshipping thru the Storm mean to you?
2. What hopes and dreams did you abandon during difficult time?
3. What steps can you take to revive those dreams?

Take time on the next few pages to record your thoughts

1. What does worshipping thru the storm mean to you?

_____

_____

_____

_____

_____

_____

_____

_____

_____

2. What hopes and dreams have you abandoned during difficult times?

_____

3. What steps can you take to revive those hopes and dreams moving forward?

_____

_____

_____

_____

_____

_____

_____

_____

Chapter Six

LOVING YOURSELF AND OTHERS THRU THE STORM

The concept of loving yourself is a simple yet complex phenomenon. Many of our downfalls are internal issues we struggle with. How do you love you – when you are your biggest problem! Self-condemnation robs so many of us from living the abundant life God intends for us. Take a moment to catch that. The key to loving YOU is trusting the love of God to make up the difference.

> *We put our hope in the Lord, He is our help and our shield. In him our hearts rejoice for we trust in his holy name. Let your unfailing love surround us Lord, for our hope is in you alone. (Psalms 33:20-22)*

This verse speaks to hope. Hope is a feeling of expectation and desire for a certain thing to happen. When we put our hope in the Lord then it gives us the fuel to love ourselves and others even in the midst of the storm. When your heart is set on the Lord, and not your circumstances, you will be able to rejoice. It's what I call the "Anyhow Praise"! Verse 22 declares *"Lord, let your love surround us for our hope is in you alone"*. God's love is surrounding you in this very moment as you are reading these words.

Going through a storm can cause a numbness. Initially you feel the effects of it, but as time goes on you become somewhat immune to what is going on in the atmosphere of your life. What I found is that, how I felt about myself would determine what I looked like after the storm. When your marriage is plagued with infidelity, the first thing you will do is look in the mirror and say "What is wrong with me?". You question if you are good enough. Self – esteem is slaughtered by guilt and shame. Resentment causes you to age faster than days are going by. Regardless of how your life has turned out you must know that you are God's unique and special creation.

Loving yourself through the storm means being reassured that God loves you. 1 John 4:8 says *"But anyone who does not love does not know God, for God is love"*. God is with you and God is love. Women especially struggle with their identity and self-esteem when they have gone through a major life upheaval. When my marriage dissolved after 10 years, I really didn't know who I was. I felt so confused about my identity and my ability to maintain a relationship. I suffered from the guilt of not being able to make things better. My ability to trust others was destroyed. Not just the ability to trust men, but the ability to trust anyone that came close to me. The storm takes away the confidence needed to build friendship and relationship. I simply didn't love myself and didn't believe that someone could genuinely love me. I can recall multiple seasons of isolation. My physical body wasn't in a dark room sleeping all day – I was active, working, taking care of my children and going about life. But my heart and soul was still in a place of isolation. Closed off from love. I thank God for my father, mother, sisters, church family, close friends. They all loved me thru my season when I truly didn't love myself. God will send you the help you need right in the midst of your storm.

Truly Job felt the struggle of being unable to love himself through the storm. Chapter 3 opens up with Job cursing the day he was born. What a low place to be in your thoughts and emotions.

> *"Let the day of my birth be erased, and the night I was conceived. Let the day be turned to darkness. Let it be lost even to God on high, and let no light shine on it." Job 3:3-4*

As I read these words, I realized Job's self-worth had diminished in his own eyes. There was an agony and pain inside that was indescribable. He was finding it hard to love himself through the storm.

Sometimes when going through a difficult time, we will try to comfort it with physical band-aids. Some people look to food as a comfort. Some people shop till they drop, so they can appear to have it all together on the outside. Some people look to promiscuity to soothe the pain. While some people simply isolate to depression and have no desire for any of the above. My challenge to you is to evaluate how you feel about yourself during the storm. What do you see when you look in the mirror? Have you noticed the sparkle in your own eye? Do you take time for yourself to ensure you get the proper rest? Are you giving your time and energy to people who don't deserve it and who are only capitalizing on your pain? Question the person who knows the best – YOU.

I'm not writing this because I have it figured out. I'm writing this because every single day I struggle to love myself through the storm. And every single day I make an effort to love myself a little more. And I see the positive effect of it. I'm able to make better choices for my life with God's direction. I can say "No" when it is necessary and not feel like I have to be a people pleaser. When I wake up and ask myself how I got here – I answer those thoughts with a positive assurance that God is walking with me. All you have is today. Yesterday is gone and tomorrow is not promised. Make a vow to love yourself today. Not for vanity, but because God is love. And if you cannot love yourself- how can you effectively love someone else? It starts on the inside of your own heart. I know your heart is broken. But you must pick up the pieces and move forward. Don't worry about the past!

> *"No, dear brothers and sisters, I have not achieved it, but I focus on this one thing: Forgetting the past and looking forward to what lies ahead" (Phillipians 4:13)*

Thoughts to Ponder:

The key to loving YOU is trusting the love of God to make up the difference.

When we put our hope in the Lord then it gives us the fuel to love ourselves and others even in the midst of the storm.

Yesterday is gone and tomorrow is not promised. Make a vow to love yourself today.

Journal Moments:

1. Write about any struggles you may have had with loving yourself thru the storm.
2. How do you feel about yourself when you look in the mirror?
3. How can you continue to make the effort to see yourself thru God's eyes?

Take time on the next few pages to record your thoughts

1. Write about any struggles you may have had with loving yourself thru the storm.

   _____

   _____

   _____

   _____

   _____

   _____

   _____

   _____

   _____

   _____

   _____

   _____

   _____

   _____

   _____

   _____

   _____

2. How do you feel about yourself when you look in the mirror?

   _____

   _____

   _____

   _____

   _____

   _____

   _____

   _____

   _____

   _____

   _____

   _____

   _____

   _____

   _____

   _____

3. How can you continue to make the effort to see yourself thru God's eyes?

_____

_____

_____

_____

_____

_____

_____

_____

_____

_____

_____

_____

_____

_____

_____

Chapter Seven

GROWING THRU THE STORM

During a painful period of my life, one day it dawned on me about the purpose of the garden hoe. The hoe is an important tool in the gardener's fight against weeds. The steel blade of the hoe sinks into the earth to remove the weeds. But it's purpose is not just to remove the weeds. The purpose of the garden hoe is also to stir the soil. The stirring of the soil promotes moisture, nutrients and growing space. What a revelation!

While I could feel the steel blade of the pain working on my heart, the purpose of the pain was not to kill me. I had to feel the pain so it could stir me up. Because of the pain it forced me to look at my life through a different lens. I realized my shortcoming and the areas where I did not guard my heart, where the issues of life flows out of. The pain stirred me up to write the words of these very pages. I knew I had to send a message to the world that the storm clouds were passing. While you may feel like you are drowning in life, it's not the final word! There is more for you!

As the soil of my heart was stirred up, it promoted moisture in my life. The moisture may have come from the rain produced by storm clouds or from the deliberate pouring in from others. Either way, the moisture has been good for my heart. Better for you to have water than to be dry. The pain also produced nutrients – some of which I have not discovered yet. Out of the pain, I have gained humility and compassion. I have walked in my shoes and can now appreciate the shoes of others. I have learned day by day how not to be bitter. I can enjoy others, laugh, pray and wish the best for even those who contributed to my pain. I embraced the concept of "due time" in every area of my life. Pain has translated to birth in my life.

I admonish you that whatever your challenges are, don't disregard the spiritual gardener in your life. Allow your mind, body, and soul to be cultivated, stirred up, moisturized and nurtured through the presence of God. If you stop and listen, you will find Him – there waiting patiently to do his gardening work in your life. The storm will only make your garden stronger. When rain falls, it is essential that there is some sort of outlet to prevent flooding. The rain has to fall, but you don't have to drown in it. As the rain pours in, you pour out. I've preached some of my most powerful messages while I was in the midst of a storm. While the issues were pouring down, God allowed me to pour out from my heart. And because of my storm, I could sense the needs of others at greater levels. Humility is one of the greatest fruits of your spiritual garden. There's a tendency to be humble during the storm, but move away from a state of humility when the storm clouds pass. But I admonish you to remain humble even when the sun is shining bright. It will allow you to stay in a place of revelation and love.

Your first inclination may be to complain during this time of your life. Job knew that all too well when he said:

> *"I cannot keep from speaking. I must express my anguish. My bitter soul must complain". Job 7:11*

It's natural to complain! I'm so grateful for my mother, father, and sisters who were so patient with me as I complained about the same things over and over again! I was like a broken record. But the issue with complaining is that as soon as I opened my mouth, any form of peace that I had vanished. I may have gone the whole day without verbalizing my anxiety, but the minute I spoke it in the atmosphere I could feel the change. Every time you decide to complain, there is a transaction that occurs in your atmosphere. Even if the storm cloud is trying move on – when I complain I am forcing it to stay lingering over me. Don't get me wrong. It is healthy to have someone to talk to about difficult situations. Talking can heal the soul. But it should be purposeful talking with solutions and even prayer to comfort.

The definition of complaining is to express grief, pain, or discontent. Those are all valid feelings. To understand further, I looked at the synonyms of the word complain on the Merriam Webster website (www.m-w.com). Some of them were: bellyache, crab, fuss, growl, grumble, moan, murmur, scream, whine and kick. I realized that these words perfectly describe how I feel when I complain! It did leave me with a bellyache at times and feeling very crabby. I'm sure you can relate to this (smile)! There were plenty of days that I looked like a baby kicking and screaming and whining as well! I found my complaining self right in the dictionary with my picture next to it!

I'm so grateful the story doesn't end there for me and you. For every word there is a synonym (a word that is exactly the same as another word). But there is also an antonym (a word that has the opposite meaning)! Which means that for every situation there is an ability to remain the same (synonym) or to change your situation (antonym) by your actions. The near antonyms for complain are accept, bear, countenance, endure, and take. As I read this, I realized that should be our countenance. Instead of complaining, we should endure. Instead of fussing, we should accept and ask for the will of God to be complete in our lives. I know these words may not be comfortable to receive right now. You may be saying, why should I accept the wrong that someone else has done? Why should I be willing to bear this storm? The reality is that there is growth in the storm.

> *"Dear brothers and sisters, when troubles of any kind come your way, consider it an opportunity for great joy. For you know that when your faith is tested, your endurance has a chance to grow. So let it grow, for when your endurance is fully developed you will be perfect and complete, needing nothing". James 1: 2-4*

This scripture is so encouraging! Read it more than once. The testing in your life right now is producing a steadfastness that you never knew you could have. And this steadfastness is the major key to you being made perfect and complete. Not perfect in the eyes of a man or woman. Rather the perfection is in the Will of God. This leaves you complete and lacking nothing. It's possible to lose everything and still lack nothing. I said to someone the other day "I've lost so much that all I can do now is be filled". Don't think of your emptiness as a negative. But see it as an opportunity to be filled with more. If you open up, you will find that you have the ability to pour out even in your toughest season. Your growth during the storm is essential. Don't remain stagnant – because your storm clouds are passing.

> ## Thoughts to Ponder:
>
> *Allow your mind, body, and soul to be cultivated, stirred up, moisturized and nurtured through the presence of God.*
>
> *Humility is one of the greatest fruits of your spiritual garden.*
>
> *Don't think of your emptiness as a negative. But see it as an opportunity to be filled with more.*

Journal Moments:

1. Have you seen any growth in yourself during difficult times? If so, what type of growth? If not, what do you think has held you back from growth?
2. Meditate and record strategies to ensure you can start growing or remain in a place of growth.
3. What is the fruit of the growth that you intend to see in your life? Come back to these thoughts periodically to ensure you are making progress!

Take time on the next few pages to record your thoughts

1. Have you seen any growth in yourself during difficult times? If so, what type of growth? If not, what do you think has held you back from growth?

_____
_____
_____
_____
_____
_____
_____
_____

_____
_____
_____
_____
_____
_____
_____

2. Meditate and record strategies to ensure you can start growing or remain in a place of growth.

_____
_____
_____
_____
_____
_____
_____
_____
_____
_____
_____
_____
_____

3. What is the fruit of the growth that you intend to see in your life? Come back to these thoughts periodically to ensure you are making progress!

_____
_____
_____
_____
_____
_____

Nikki Henderson

Chapter Eight

YOU'VE SIGHED LONG ENOUGH – IT'S TIME FOR YOU TO CRY OUT!

At the start of 2017, I decided it was a "back to basics" year for me. I wanted to spend more time exploring God's word and listening for the still small voice of God like never before. When you are in the midst of the storm, it's possible to become too busy to even pray at times. You are so busy talking and so busy trying to solve problems. But it is really in the word of God, that you find that rest. As I began this journey, I decided to revisit reading the bible over a course of a year again.

The book of Exodus, Chapter 2 begins with the birth of Moses amidst a call to kill all firstborn males by placing them in the river. There was a summons sent out by Pharaoh to destroy all the Hebrew babies. But Moses' mother looks on him and saw he was special. And she put him in the river, but in a basket so he would not drown. While the command was to allow Moses to drown, his mother did what she could to protect him even in the waves of life. Moses was in the middle of a storm and didn't even know it. There are people who will see your potential in the midst of the storm, and seek strategies to ensure you don't drown. Like Moses, it may be a parent who tried to advise you to not to make certain decisions. And even though you went your own way, they covered you in a basket of prayer.

Ironically, Moses lands right into the arms of Pharaoh's daughter and she had compassion on him and she brought Moses into Pharaoah's house and raised him there. Exodus 2:23 -25 takes us to the next phase of this account:

> *"Years passed, and the King of Egypt died. But the Isrealites continued to groan under their burden of slavery. They cried out for help, and their cry rose up to God. God heard their groaning, and he remembered his covenant promise in Abraham, Isaac, and Jacob. He looked down on the people of Isreal and knew it was time to act".*

One early morning as I read this account, these words stood out to me – process of time.

I felt like there was more for me to ponder there. So I began to dig deeper. A process is a systemic series of actions directed to some end. In other words, no matter what I am going through, there is an end date. Your stormy season is really just your process. And it's not meant to last forever. It's not meant to go on into Infinity as it relates to time. There is a process for everything. Meat on the shelf at your local supermarket has to be processed before you can buy it. Gold is purified through a process of high temperature or chemical exposure.

On the other hand, time is the indefinite continued progress of existence and events in the past, present, and future regarded as a whole. When my human mind tries to calculate time, it is not limited to just one segment. For example, mentally last week and this week is all one segment in the overall principle of time. As I pondered on these two separate and distinct definitions, I realized that process of time means there is a systemic series of actions that must come to an expected end within this indefinite existence (think on that for a moment).

Because of the process of time, you may feel like you can't make it through your circumstances because your process is in the middle of something your mind cannot measure. That's why God says "Your ways are not my ways and your thoughts are not my thoughts". While time is indefinite, God allows process to connect with time so that there can be an expected end! So I'm here to serve notice to the one who just said to the issues in your life that it seems they will never go away. There is a process in time for your deliverance and it's here and now! Nobody can sit you down from praising God because you have endured your process in time! The systematic series of events - good, bad, or ugly are only driving you to the place where God hears your cry.

The death of the King of Egypt sets off the Children of Isreal's process to their deliverance. His death caused them to consider their current state. This moment of deliverance in the Exodus of the Children of Isreal is a powerful concept that you must embrace in the midst of your storm. There has to be a trigger moment in your life in which you stop to consider where you are. You have to ask the question – where am I and how did I get here? And most importantly – where am I going? The Children of Isreal struggled in bondage for many years but the day came for their Exodus. Exodus means to depart and exit. What steps are you taking to depart and exit your storm? If you are having a financial storm, what changes have you made to prepare for the release from the bondage? If your relationships are in the middle of a storm, what strategies are you focusing on to see your way through? It so easy to identify the storm, but sometimes it is extremely difficult to identify when the storm is passing.

As I read this account, my eyes were opened to a spiritual formula for prayer encased in these two scriptures. The Lord laid this revelation on my heart while I prepared to preach at a prayer conference being hosted by my church. Exodus 2:23 in the King James Bible version says, "And the Children of Isreal sighed by reason of the bondage". It's interesting that the Bible describes it that way because to sigh means to emit a long, deep, audible, breath expressing sadness, relief, tiredness or a similar feeling. The Hebrew meaning of sigh in this context is to groan in pain or grief. They finally came to the point of enough is enough! Have you ever been in that place where you felt like enough was enough?

From a natural perspective, when you breathe out, or exhale, your diaphragm relaxes and moves upward into the chest cavity. The intercostal muscles between the ribs also relax to reduce the space in the chest cavity. As the space in the chest cavity gets smaller, air rich in carbon dioxide is forced out of your lungs and windpipe, and then out of your nose or mouth. It is a good thing to exhale, but some of us are just sighing at the issues going on in our lives. We're frustrated but we aren't saying anything to God. We don't know how long the Children of Isreal groaned in pain but we know it was significant enough to be called out as a stage in the process to their deliverance.

The next portion of this verse declares – *"They cried out for help and their cry rose up to God"*. This cry was a cry for help. It was their cry that came up unto God. Now, at last, they began to think of God under their troubles, and to return to him from the idols they had served. But before God unbound them he put it into their hearts to cry unto him. It is a good sign that God is coming towards us with deliverance when he inclines and enables us to cry to him for it. We have to cry out to God in this season. In order for bondage to be removed and for the storm clouds to pass, there must be a cry!

Exodus 2:24 declares *"God heard their groaning"*. This portion of scripture struck a chord with me because it was very distinct and clear that God heard their cry. It was not overlooked by the Most High God. There have been times when I cried out and I could sense the confirmation that it was heard by the Lord. The Hebrew word for heard is Shaw-mah, which means to listen, obey, to grant request. It also means "sound". It was in their cry that God then could hear their pain. Sound is a vibration that transforms itself as an audible mechanical wave of pressure and displacement, through a transmission medium such as air or water.

Sound is then the reception of the waves and the perception by the brain. You hear by the way of sound and it is happening faster than you can even receive the words. There was a distinct sound raised to heaven – all God heard was the cry.

The transmission of the Children of Isreal's cry to heaven caused God to remember his covenant with Abraham, with Isaac, and with Jacob. In Genesis 12 God made a covenant with Abraham that he would make him a great nation and bless him and make his name great. And not only that he would be blessed but that all the families of the earth would be blessed. Next, in Genesis 26 God made a covenant with Isaac that he would be with him and bless him and give him countries and allow his seed to multiply. God further grants covenant with Jacob in Genesis 28 telling him he will be kept in all the places he goes and that God will never leave him. Their cry activated the promises of God that had been spoken on generations past.

God heard the cry of the Children of Isreal and he looked upon them. Man can look at your situation and feel bad for you and even make attempts to soothe you. But when God looks upon you, there is a help from on high that comes in the middle of your storm. Holding on in the storm means you have to be willing to cry out. This is your clarion call to cry out to God.

You have sighed long enough – God is ready to hear your heart cry. He knows your situation but He wants to hear it from you. It doesn't have to be a dramatic cry. It could simply be you sharing your true feelings with God in a quiet place. Tell God how you <u>really</u> feel. He's heard from my mother but what about me? He's heard your grandmother on your behalf but what about you? Are you simply looking up at the storm clouds and seeking shelter hoping it will pass. Or are you running out in the storm and crying out to Heaven for a shift in your life? You've sighed long enough!

Thoughts to Ponder:

There are people who will see your potential in the midst of the storm, and seek strategies to ensure you don't drown.

There has to be a trigger moment in your life in which you stop to consider where you are.

You have sighed long enough – God is ready to hear your heart cry.

Journal Moments:

1. Ask yourself the questions: Where am I? How did I get here? Where am I going?
2. When was the last time you actually cried? How did it feel?
3. Take time to meditate and write the words of your heart regarding your situation – allow your words to activate change through your heart cry.

Take time on the next few pages to record your thoughts

1. Ask yourself the questions: Where am I? How did I get here? Where am I going?

_____
_____
_____
_____
_____
_____
_____
_____
_____
_____
_____
_____

_____
_____
_____

2. When was the last time you actually cried? How did it feel?

_____
_____
_____
_____
_____
_____
_____
_____
_____
_____
_____
_____
_____

3. Take time to meditate and write the words of your heart regarding your situation – allow your words to activate change through your heart cry.

_____
_____
_____
_____
_____
_____
_____
_____
_____
_____
_____
_____
_____

Chapter Nine

BE CAREFUL WHO YOU LISTEN TO DURING THE STORM

There are storms which show up in our lives and we may not have a trace of them at all except for the rain. I think of those as quiet storms. You may be able to appear normal and it may seem on the surface that everything is going ok. Only you really know the storm you were in the midst of. It could be a quiet storm of loneliness after loss of a spouse, or divorce. It's the quiet intimate struggles that you don't even verbalize in prayer – but they exist.

Then on the other hand, there are thunderstorms that show up in our lives like Job experienced (Job 1 – 2). These types of storms are very transparent for others to see, and we even change with them. Job 2:7-8 gives the account of Job being smote with boils all over his body by Satan. A boil is a skin infection that is characterized by hard lumps. Just one boil is painful – imagine Job having boils all over his body! He was in absolute anguish. He attempted to find relief with a potsherd, which is a broken fragment of pottery. I can imagine Job having beautiful pottery because he was so well off. In his time of distress, he used a broken piece of pottery to scrape his boils with hope of relief. I believe this potsherd symbolized the state he was in during his storm.

As I read this, I tried to visualize Job in a painful state with boils. And then I further tried to visualize Job using this broken piece of pottery in order to scrape his boils. I began to question Job as if I was there with him " Job, why are you using pain to relieve pain?". This may sound like a rhetorical question, but in essence Job was applying pain in order to relieve pain!

The Bible is very specific in pointing out this act that Job is performing on himself. It doesn't say he went to get a healing salve and he wrapped up the boils. Nor does it say he found a warm stream to relieve the pain. Instead, he scraped his skin and sat in ashes. More pain!

That's when I caught the revelation that many of us do this very thing. Picture yourself in the midst of a difficult time in your life. Take a moment and visualize that season whether it is now or in the past. Now, these next few words will require an honest look within. In your difficult season, have you focused on healing your situation or do you apply more pain? If you chose a certain type of man or woman in your past relationship and it caused you so much pain – why do we still choose the same type of person again? Why do we apply pain to pain that already exists? If you struggled with your finances and it landed you in a storm – have you noticed that sometimes through your actions your situation may get worse before it gets better?

If you struggle with self-esteem and identity, then you can't look yourself in the mirror everyday and criticize yourself. That's only applying pain to pain! You are scraping the very pain points in your life. In my role as a leader in Corporate America, I have done exercises in order to identify what we call "points of pain". These are in essence operational issues in which we may be struggling with in my department. It may not seem worthwhile to have a meeting just to identify painful things. It's actually very uncomfortable because it requires a level of transparency in order to get to a place of solution. If I am not willing to expose and talk about the things that make it difficult to operate – then I cannot move towards problem solving.

What I have found with this exercise of identifying "points of pain", is that sometimes things are being handled in a way that is contradictive to the proper workflow. So for example, a point of pain I may possibly identify may be "We don't have enough money in our budget to hire new staff and meet our goals". This may seem like a reasonable and common point of pain. But when you dig deeper, there may be staff members that are underperforming. And with some focus on development, I could bring the current staff up to another level and not require any additional hiring. So it's important to identify the pain point and then look for solutions.

Job sat in ashes as a sign of grief, humility, and penitence which is regret for sin and wrong doing. Job went into a position of humility and regret although he knew he had lived righteous in the sight of God. Instead of blaming God, Job decided to look inward. There are some who will very quickly sit in the ashes when life begins to turn upside down. Others will refuse to accept that they had any part in the circumstances at hand. Job humbled himself before God.

As Job is going through his trials, I would have hoped he had a supportive wife on his side. But it turns out that is not the case. Job's wife approaches him in the middle of his trial with these words:

> *"Are you still trying to maintain your integrity? Curse God and die." Job 2: 9*

What strong words to hear from your spouse in the middle of your storm! Your husband or wife should be the one to know your heart the most. And it may appear she is a villain in this context. But I also pictured her as someone who was hurting watching her husband in so much pain. She felt that there was peace in death at this point in Moses's situation. Sometimes it is those who are the closest to us that will struggle with our pain the most. And they may not know how to appropriately support you through the storm.

There are times when crisis arises and your spouse may not be able to comfort you. Your best friend may not be able to walk with you either. These are the times where you must seek God on your own and listen to his voice. It's tempting to add pain to pain – even for others that we expect comfort from. The key is that we must be in tune with what is going on around us in order to help someone through the storm. I find that it is so easy to miss things on a day to day basis. Possibly your children or spouse may come home after a bad day at work or school – but because of your own worries you may not be able to support them. Your spouse may listen as you express your pain – but give advice out of anger. This is in essence what Job's wife did. Her response was out of a place of her own pain. Remember – she just lost everything as Job lost everything because she was connected to him. Possibly she was in a place of deciding to curse God.

Be mindful of who you receive your advice from during the storm. Take a moment to evaluate where that person is at that moment. Are they also in a place of loss and grief? Because most likely that is the place where they will only be able to provide support from. Have you ever called someone to tell them about your problem and then they begin to tell you about their problem? And then by the time you hang up – you are more depressed than you were before you called them! It doesn't mean that we avoid others because they are going through as well. Rather we change the focus of the interaction to one of building up and encouragement. For example, if we are both experiencing difficulty in a similar area, we spend time reading the Bible in relation to the issue we are having together and pray about it.

As a mom of two boys who are both 10 and under, I struggle with patience sometimes! I want them to sit still, clean up, stop arguing, and everything else that normal boys do! When I find my patience is wearing thin, I get out the concordance and look for all scriptures related to patience and read them. This helps me feed my spirit with positive thoughts and advice rather than complaining. Who you listen to and what you feed into your spirit is very important during a stormy period of life.

Thoughts to Ponder:

If you struggle with self-esteem and identity, then you can't look yourself in the mirror everyday and criticize yourself. That's only applying pain to pain!

Sometimes it is those who are the closest to us that will struggle with our pain the most.

Be mindful of who you receive your advice from during the storm.

Journal Moments:

1. In your difficult season, have you focused on healing your situation or do you apply more pain?
2. Who is the strongest voice in your life to provide advice and why?
3. How will you ensure you are not applying pain to the already painful points in your life?

   Take time on the next few pages to record your thoughts

1. In your difficult season, have you focused on healing your situation or do you apply more pain?

   _____
   _____
   _____
   _____
   _____
   _____
   _____

_____
_____
_____
_____
_____
_____
_____
_____

2. Who is the strongest voice in your life to provide advice and why?

_____
_____
_____
_____
_____
_____
_____
_____
_____
_____
_____
_____
_____
_____

3. How will you ensure you are not applying pain to the already painful points in your life?

_____
_____
_____
_____
_____
_____
_____

Nikki Henderson

_____
_____
_____
_____
_____
_____
_____

Chapter Ten

YOUR RESPONSE IS CRITICAL DURING THE STORM

Your response to what you hear is just as important as who you listen to. I've always heard the saying "Think before you act". More importantly is think before you speak. How we respond during the stormy season of our life is just as important because it sets the stage for the outcome. If you are easily triggered, your stress levels with be through the roof. We can't let our buttons be pushed so easily by the fiery darts of the devil! You must be able to stand strong in the Lord and in the power of HIS MIGHT! In the prior chapter we talked about Job's wife and and how she questioned his loyalty. I love the fact that the story of Job's faith does not stop there.

Job did not sit and ponder what his wife said and consider cursing God. Sometimes we sit and ponder thoughts too long that go against what we know God desires for us. We all have received some form of negative feedback, whether it be a doctor's report indicating sickness or disappointment by someone we love. When we receive these reports it is easy to ponder and wallow in worry, anxiety, and even regret. But in some instances we need an instant God inspired response to the storm. Job's response was beyond imagination!

> *"But Job replied, "You talk like a foolish woman. Should we accept only good things from the hand of God and never anything bad?" So in all of this, Job said nothing wrong".* *Job 2:10*

Read Job's response a second time before continuing. Now I need to remind you of Job's current state. He has lost everything, including his children. At this time he has boils all over his body and is using broken pottery to scrape them along with sitting in ashes. Picture Job in this state. And out of his brokenness, he has enough strength to not only rebuke his wife's comment but to question whether we should only accept good, and no bad. What an interesting question for him to point out! Many of us struggle with this same concept. It's easy to accept the mountaintop but difficult to journey through the desert. There are high times and low times in this life. How we respond is the absolute key to our breakthrough.

The scripture then declares that in all of this, Job said nothing wrong. It was already mind-boggling that Job was able to question his wife's state of mind during his storm but at the same time the Bible declares that in all of this , Job said nothing wrong. These four words stood out to me "In all of this". Many of us are right of the middle of an "In all of this" storm. There are so many real struggles that you have to deal and contend with on a daily basis. "In all of this" sums up all of the hurt, pain, disappointment and loss you have experienced into four words. My only concern is that I may have the "In all of this" season active in my life – classified as a storm. But can someone write the story about me and say the next few words – "Job said nothing wrong"?

Ask yourself how you are responding to the storms in your life. When you feel like "In all of this" is evident in your life and the cares are weighing you down – how are you responding? Are you allowing depression to be your response? Are thoughts of suicide and ending it all ruling in your life? Truly there were days that I struggled with simply getting out of the bed. My heart was so heavy. But the reminder that the storm clouds were passing was a prescription for my thought process. You have to begin to respond in a way that is pleasing to God. Respond in faith.

Be careful what you say during the storm. When we speak out of distress or anger, there are things said which cannot be recovered. If a child is told they are not smart, they will tend to manifest that in their lives. Simply because of what was spoken. How you respond to others will be key during this season of your life. You must stand flat-footed in faith and speak out of a place of faith. Jesus gave his disciples this very direction in Matthew 17:20:

> *"You don't have enough faith," Jesus told them. "I tell you the truth, if you had faith even as small as a mustard seed, you could say to this mountain, 'Move from here to there,' and it would move. Nothing would be impossible." Matthew 17:20*

Mustard seeds are one of the smallest seeds you can find! Yet they are a key source of oil and protein. And they only take about 3-10 days to germinate if placed in the right conditions. So in other words, they are small and don't take long to grow!! When you are going through, your faith may be just like a mustard seed – small and needing to accelerate in growth quickly. But it's in these times that faith becomes evident and all the more vital.

When you receive a negative report or it all looks dark, you have to begin to speak in faith to move the mountains. Your bills are due but your income is cut short – this is a time to speak in faith. Don't die in the winter. Hold fast to God's unchanging hand. In due time, you will see the storm clouds passing. You've spent enough time being angry during the storm, now try to focus on prayer for breakthrough. I have made a conscious decision to stop complaining. There are times where it may slip through. But the reality is that no matter how much I complain, it won't change the circumstances in my life. Sometimes the change is right there inside of me. When I begin to speak differently about my life, I am setting myself up for change.

II Kings 4 shares the account of Elisha and the woman from Shunem. Elisha was a prophet and was successor to another important prophet Elijah. Every time that Elisha traveled to Shunem, there was a wealthy woman there and her family who prepared a place for Elisha. He came there enough, that she spoke with her husband and decided to build him a small room that he could rest in whenever he visited. On one of his visits, Elisha asked for the woman to be sent to him to ask her if there was something he could do for her because of her kindness. She gracefully told Elisha that she was not in need of anything because her family took good care of her. After she left, Elisha asked Gehazi, his trusted servant if there was something he could do for this woman from Shunem. Elisha was not letting her get off so easily without receiving a blessing.

Gehazi had been observing the woman's life and he realized that she didn't have a son and her husband was an old man. So there was barrenness in her life. Although she had all of the material wealth, she did not have a child. Based on her initial response, she may have been in a state of giving up on having a child. But when Elisha called her back he told her that in the next year at that time she will be holding a son in her arms - she responded by saying *"No, my lord!" she cried. "O man of God, don't deceive me and get my hopes up like that." 2 Kings 4:15.* Based on her response, she had hopes before but had given up. There was something she desired but too afraid to hope for.

God fulfilled the word spoken by Elisha and she gave birth to a child by the next year at that same time. But one day when the child is older, he begins to complain that his head hurts and his mother held him in her lap and by noon he passed away. I can only imagine the pain and distress she felt. Truly this was her storm! Her response to the storm was mind-boggling! She laid her son down on the bed and told her husband to send a servant with a donkey so she could go to find Elisha. When she approached Elisha, she fell to the ground and grabbed hold of his feet and cried out regarding her hopes of her child. But she wasn't in a state of giving up – instead she demanded that Elisha go to her house to see about her son. The account ends with Elisha praying for her son and he was raised back to life.

While you may not have the same storm that this woman experienced – I'm driving home the thought of evaluating how you respond to your storm. How you react will be key to the final outcome. Will you just die in the storm? Or will you cry out and fight for life to be restored in your life? The choice is yours.

Even Job struggled with his thoughts during his time of distress and he complained and even cursed the day that he was born. But he was mindful of what he would say and acknowledged that by saying:

> *"At least I can take comfort in this; Despite the pain, I have not denied the words of the Holy One". Job 6:10*

Job made it a point to ensure that despite what he was going through he could still be in the right place with God because of his response to the storm. Take the time to evaluate your response during the storm.

<u>Thoughts to Ponder:</u>

Your response to what you hear is just as important as who you listen to.

It's easy to accept the mountaintop but difficult to journey through the desert.

How you react will be key to the final outcome.

Journal Moments:

1. What has been your response to the storms that come in your life?
2. How does your life reflect your response?
3. If there is something you can change or enhance about the way your respond to difficult times – what would it be? How will you incorporate this change going forward?

   ### *Take time on the next few pages to record your thoughts*

1. What has been your response to the storms that come in your life?

   _____
   _____
   _____
   _____
   _____
   _____
   _____
   _____
   _____
   _____
   _____
   _____
   _____
   _____
   _____
   _____

2. How does your life reflect your response?

   _____
   _____
   _____
   _____
   _____
   _____
   _____
   _____

_____
_____
_____
_____
_____
_____
_____

3. If there is something you can change or enhance about the way your respond to difficult times – what would it be? How will you incorporate this change going forward?

_____
_____
_____
_____
_____
_____
_____
_____
_____
_____
_____
_____
_____

Chapter Eleven

FORGIVENESS DURING AND AFTER THE STORM

This may have been the hardest chapter to write in the entire book – forgiveness. Forgiveness does not come naturally. It is a conscious decision that you make to release the pain, guilt, shame – whatever it is that has you bound. What is forgiveness? It is your <u>act and attitude</u> towards those who have wronged you. Sometimes we say we forgive from our mouths but our attitude and the way we behave does not line up with that declaration. Jesus taught the importance of forgiveness in the Lord's prayer by saying *"and forgive us our sins, as we have forgiven those who sin against us"* (Matthew 6:12). We need the divine act of forgiveness for our own lives. Truly I am just a sinner saved by grace! I've made mistakes, mishaps, and misroutes in my life and it's the grace of the Forgiveness of God that allows me to be able to write the words on these pages. It's nothing that I have earned – forgiveness is a gift to me. But although I know that in the crevices of my soul, it can still be difficult to forgive in this human heart and mind.

When your heart is broken, I picture the pieces shattered like a glass. And there are storms that come in our life and literally break our hearts. These types of storms usually involve others. It may be a family member, spouse, or even child. But there is some damage that occurs. I have seen families go through storms and never speak to each other again. They may have spent their entire lives together sharing a room, playing and eating together – and one storm destroys the relationship and fellowship. While on the surface they may feel as if they don't need the other individual in their life, there may be a piece of them missing. On the other hand, some of our storms were caused by people we were never meant to connect with anyway.

The storm passes over but we are still not whole. I'm here to submit a key piece of being whole as you prepare for the storm clouds to pass. You need to forgive more now like never before. Forgiveness does not mean you give the person a "pass". It means you let go and let God. Forgiveness is vital in your healing process.

I want to introduce you to a man named Joseph in the Bible. He is a true example of how the ability to forgive opens the doors to fellowship and relationships. The restoration of fellowship is not always with the person who hurt you. The restoration may come in the form of new relationships. And because of forgiveness, you are able to be open to others. Holding the pain in your heart blocks you from trusting others. I lost count of the numerous potential friendships I missed because I was in the middle of my storm and unable to let anyone in. Take note of Joseph's story.

The book of Genesis introduces us to Isreal's son, Joseph, in Chapter 37. Joseph at the time of the setting is seventeen years old and he was feeding the flock with his brothers. The Bible gives the account that Isreal loved Joseph more than his other sons. And because of this, Joseph's brothers hated him. Here we have the onset of a storm fueled by jealousy. To complicate matters further – Joseph has a dream that he and his brothers are binding sheaves in the field and his sheaf arose and stood upright, while their sheaves stood around him and bowed down to his sheaf. In his dream, it is harvest time and he and his brothers are binding up corn to bring home. His corn stands erect on its own while their corn bows down. Truly this only made the sibling rivalry worse! He has another similar dream and tells his father and brothers. Even his father is surprised by the implications of the dream and questions Joseph.

> *"This time he told the dream to his father as well as to his brothers, but his father scolded him. "What kind of dream is that?" he asked. "Will your mother and I and your brothers actually come and bow to the ground before you?"* **(Genesis 37:10).**

And while this only sparks envy for his brothers – vs. 11 states "his father observed the saying". He knew that there was something greater to what Joseph was seeing.

But there was one additional element that brought on the storm in Joseph's life – his coat of many colors made by his father. This coat symbolized his distinction among his brethren.

Finally they conspired to kill him but there was one brother Reuben who pleaded not to shed his blood but suggested they put him in a pit in the wilderness instead. Joseph was stripped of his coat and thrown into an empty pit with no water. Dark with nothing to nourish him. The brothers conspired further and decided Joseph was to be sold to merchantmen for twenty pieces of silver. The brothers staged Joseph's murder and brought his blood-stained coat home to his father who mourned for his favorite son who was gone.

Joseph ends up in Egypt and goes from the pit where his brothers threw him, to the palace of Potiphar who is an office of Pharoah, the Ruler of the Land. Joseph prospers well but a set-up and wrongful accusation by Potiphar's wife lands Joseph in prison. Surely Joseph has to be feeling the weight of his storm. He had spent his younger years being faithful to his family and was forsaken. He did all he could to please Potiphar and make the best of his new home – and now once again he is forsaken. I'm sure you can think of storms in your life, where you did all the "right things" but you still seem to go from the pit to the palace and back to prison. It's a cyclical storm which seems to give you moments of relief only to come raging in again.

I'm so grateful that Joseph's story doesn't end there. Although he ends up in prison, there is a still a blessing on him to prosper. What I love about the flow of life, is that when God has placed a blessing over your life, it doesn't matter where you end up. The blessing is still there over you.

> *"But the Lord was with Joseph in the prison and showed him his faithful love. And the Lord made Joseph a favorite with the prison warden." (Geneis 39:21)*

Despite his storm, the Lord was with him and that is the message that you must grasp in your heart. I'm sure that when Joseph sat in his prison cell he didn't spend all his days smiling. The human heart and mind has the innate tendency to feel sadness when you are betrayed and when life simply appears to have dealt you a bad hand. But I pray that you will be conscious of the signs of God being WITH YOU as you go through the storm. As I look back over my life, I went through 15 years of a broken marriage, premature babies being born, divorce, and single parenting. All the while, God gave me the strength and showed me favor on my job. I was not only able to maintain my career with the same organization, but I experienced 3 promotions! This was a clear sign of God being WITH ME in the storm.

So let's go back to look at Joseph's journey in prison. Joseph's gift of dreaming follows him to prison – except this time he is not the dreamer. He is the interpreter of the dream. This amazed me because initially we think of Joseph as the dreamer but his gift to dream elevates in the process of his storm. He is now able to interpret the dreams of others through God's insight. Who you are at the beginning is not who you will be at the end! There will be a greater anointing on your life! Greater Worship! More Power! What you are going through does not diminish the hope of your future. There is greater elevation ahead!

Joseph interprets the dream of Pharaoh's butler and baker in the prison with precision and accuracy. Although the butler's dream is favorable to him, he forgets Joseph and another 2 years passes by with Joseph in prison.

"Two full years later, Pharoah dreamed…"

This is Joseph's moment and he doesn't even know it! The scripture specifically points out the fact that it was at the <u>end </u>of two full years. To every season there is an end. And Pharaoh needs an interpreter. Little does he know a <u>prisoner</u> will be the voice of God for him. He hears about Joseph and calls for him and Joseph is able to interpret the dreams which were a forewarning of seven years of plenty in the land of Egypt followed by seven years of famine. Joseph gives Pharaoh the instruction to gather all the food from the good years and store in the city so that when the famine comes they will not perish. Pharaoh sees the Spirit of God in Joseph and says unto Joseph:

> *"Since God has revealed the meaning of the dreams to you, clearly no one else is as intelligent or wise as you are. You will be in charge of my court, and all my people will take orders from you. Only I, sitting on my throne, will have a rank higher than yours". (Genesis 41:37)*

What an amazing turn of events for Joseph! He now goes from the <u>prison </u>back to the <u>palace</u>. He rules under Pharaoh and is the orchestrator of storing up during the good years in preparation for the famine. When the famine hits the land, it is great and difficult for all those outside of Egypt.

And this is where Joseph's past connects with his future and where he speaks the final verdict over his storm. Because of the famine in the land, his brothers who had forsaken him, must now come and bow at his feet in order to get food for their family. His dream which he could only dream at seventeen – was now being interpreted by the cycle of life and time. Joseph recognizes his brothers but does not reveal himself to them on their first encounter. He asks about their family - particularly his brother Benjamin and he tells them to return with their family. It is upon return that Jacob is no longer able to contain himself because of the joy he felt in being reunited with his family. Genesis 45 opens up with the account of Joseph telling everyone to leave except his brethren and he makes himself known to them. And Joseph wept so loud that the Egyptians and the house of Pharaoh could hear him.

I suspect that Joseph cried out of his place of pain where he dwelt for so many years. He probably could never tell anyone his true story. He was bound to his past and future at the same time. But on this day, with the very brothers who initiated the storm in his life – he wept. So loud that all could hear him. Have you ever really cried from the heart of your true pain? I'm talking to woman, man, boy or girl. There is no distinction. There is a cry that comes from the very root of everything you have experienced. That causes you to cry out in earnest.

> **After Joseph cried, he told them who he was – and even thanked them for the storm.** *"Please come closer", he said to them. So they came closer. And he said again, "I am Joseph, your brother, whom you sold into slavery in Egypt. But don't be upset, and don't be angry with yourself for selling me to this place. It was God who sent me here ahead of you to preserve your lives"* (Genesis 45:4-5)

In that moment, Joseph realized that he had to go through his storm. And he was so overwhelmed by the revelation of the purpose of his storm. When he was placed into that pit as a young man it really didn't make sense to him. He felt forsaken and forgotten. But in this moment he realized that he had to go through what he went through in order to save the lives of others – even the very ones that threw him into the pit. His brothers initiated the storm in his life, but in God's ultimate plan, Joseph's storm saved their lives. I can only imagine their faces as they realized that Joseph's dream really came true. They ultimately had to bow to him during that time of famine symbolizing the sheaf that Joseph saw in his dream. How humbling and also afraid of his revenge they must have been.

Joseph could have gone into "I told you so mode". He could have gotten on his high horse and made them feel low. But Joseph had a God-inspired infusion of forgiveness and it poured out in his tears and his actions. The story would have ended differently if Joseph didn't have the ability to forgive. Forgiveness allows you to grasp the purpose of your storm. Forgiveness frees your mind to be able to meditate on positive rather than negative. What do you think about most? Because whatever is on your mind the most – that is what will manifest in your daily life.

Although I had read this story about Joseph before, it came to life to me this time in a way it has never before. I always focused on Joseph's journey from the <u>pit to the palace</u> as his triumph. But as I read it at the start of this year, I realized the real triumph came when Joseph became thankful for his storm through his very own expression of forgiveness to his brothers telling them "It's ok. I had to go through this for a bigger purpose". That was the real moral to his story.

My brother, my sister – I can assure you that there will come a time when you will sense the clear revelation of why you went through your storms in life. When you come to that place, like Joseph , you may someday look at the same people or circumstances that hurt you and say" Don't feel bad anymore – it was good that this happened". It is in that moment that true forgiveness steps into your heart and mind. When you become thankful, it counteracts against grudges, regrets, depression and hopelessness. And then your heart and mind can begin to embrace a new perspective. Is it possible that your storm could be propelling you forward? While it feels like life is going in reverse, what if God is just moving you forward?

This revelation lingered in my spirit for over a week and while standing waiting for the train, I had this "Joseph" moment for my own life. And I realized that my pain from life's storms has propelled me to a place in God that I never knew I could reach. It's a place where I feel so intimately close with God because I learned him as God the Healer. Only he could wipe my tears away. There was no replacement- I had to depend on him. And it's in that moment I could hear the small still voice speaking to my spirit right there on the train track - "Stop feeling like you lost something, instead thank me for what you gained". And I realized then, I had to remain thankful through and for the storm.

There are God-ordained storms that come into our lives like Job & Joseph. Experiences that push us to the limit in our faith. The day of victory is when you realize that if God brought you to it – He can bring you through it. Don't wait till the storm is over – be thankful now! And while you are at it – Don't forget to forgive the most important person: YOURSELF.

> ## <u>Thoughts to Ponder:</u>
>
> *When God has placed a blessing over your life, it doesn't matter where you end up. The blessing is still there over you.*
>
> *Forgiveness allows you to grasp the purpose of your storm.*
>
> *How you react will be key to the final outcome.*

Journal Moments:

1. Identify at least one grudge you know you have held about something that occurred in your life? If needed, sit before God in quiet prayer so it can be revealed to you?
2. How did that situation affect you? How does it feel when you think about it now?
3. Make a conscious decision to forgive by writing your own declaration of forgiveness. Take action to bring the forgiveness to life.

Take time on the next few pages to record your thoughts

1. Identify at least one grudge you know you have held about something that occurred in your life? If needed, sit before God in quiet prayer so it can be revealed to you?

_____

_____

_____

_____

_____
_____
_____
_____
_____
_____
_____
_____
_____
_____

2. How did that situation affect you? How does it feel when you think about it now?

_____
_____
_____
_____
_____
_____
_____
_____
_____
_____
_____
_____
_____
_____
_____

3. Make a conscious decision to forgive by writing your own declaration of forgiveness. Take action to bring the forgiveness to life.

_____
_____
_____
_____

_____
_____
_____
_____
_____
_____
_____
_____
_____
_____
_____
_____

Chapter Twelve

REST ASSURE THE
STORM WILL PASS

As I write the final pages of this book, I am in Selma, North Carolina. The purpose of my trip was to step away from my everyday routine so I could finish this work in progress. At this time, it's been almost two years from the time I grabbed hold of these words – "Storm Clouds" are Passing". Those four words ignited change in my life like never before. And it gave birth to this book. When I first saw the words, it was hard for me to believe that there would be a day that the storm clouds would pass. I couldn't imagine not waking up everyday feeling so broken inside. I wondered what life would look like. What it was like to be whole. What it would be like to be genuinely happy. How it would feel to laugh and smile.

There were moments that I felt happy – but it would wear off pretty quickly. Just one thought about my past and I would fall into the slump again. But then I realized that God really wanted me to have a new life. My past was simply that – the past. All I have is today, and tomorrow is not promised. I began to rest on scriptures like 1 Corinthians 5:17:

> *"This means that anyone who belongs to Christ has become a new person. The old life is gone: a new life has begun".*

The fact that I belong to Christ means that I have become new. And that's when the storm clouds pass- when I embrace the new life offered by Jesus Christ. My physical circumstances may not have changed much, but my heart changed and that is when the storm clouds shifted. I realized I kept the storm around longer than it was supposed to be. I actually became dependent on the storm. The storm allowed me to be victim rather than me having to step up and fight to be the victor.

I want to assure you that there is a day that you can wake up and say "It's ok, it is well with my soul". No matter what you have been through, there is an opportunity to heal and see some more sunny days in your life. Stop holding on to your past. Stop holding on to guilt and shame.

Let go of regret. The longer you mourn what you cannot change – the longer the storm clouds remain. All you have is today. If you dare to live again – God will meet you right where you are. And he will send others to celebrate your victory of coming through the storm. There is someone waiting to comfort you because of the trials you came through. But you have to make a decision to push through it first.

> *"When Job prayed for his friends, the Lord restored his fortunes (Job 42:9)*

The loneliest place for Job was during his storm. But when he came through, his family and friends were able to come to comfort and console him because he made it through! And on top of that they brought him gifts!

As my storm clouds were passing, I realized how many valuable relationships I lost during my storm. It's natural to isolate from others when you are going through. There are some special people who were very close to me that walked with me through the storm – my mom, dad, sisters, and my Pastor and his wife, and some close friends. They were allowed to see me as I was drenched in the rain of pain. But in the course of it, I lost friendships that meant a lot to me before I got into the state I was in. As I have come out of my stormy period, God has strategically orchestrated divine encounters for me to reconnect with people I lost and renew relationships. And the gift they bring are unconditional love and friendship. Something that money can never buy. Because of God's restoration in my life, I was given the honor of receiving such a beautiful foreward from one of the greatest women I have ever met, Joy Fields.

Possibly there are some things you lost during the storm. Ask God to recover those areas of your life. He will hear and grant your request. Your best days are ahead. This does not mean that you will never go through anything again. Rest assure as long as there are life, there will be trials we must come through. But you now have a recipe for success and a reminder that storm clouds do pass.

> *"Rejoice in our confident hope. Be patient in trouble, and keep on praying" Romans 12:12*

At the start of this book, I shared the story of my sons identifying the clouds in the sky almost 2 years ago. I couldn't appreciate the identification of clouds at that time. I was feeling like I was in the middle of a storm. But the amazing part about clouds is they exist, even when the sun is shining. As we took a road trip to North Carolina this weekend, the subject of clouds ironically came up in the car again as me and my two boys rode down Interstate 95 South.

Except this time, Joshua said "Mommy , look at the clouds! It looks like a man with his hands wide open". I tried to keep my eyes on the road and look up in the sky at the same time. Sure enough the clouds did appear to be a large man with arms wide open. Perhaps it was my son's childish imagination and my wishful thinking. But I saw it as a sign to confirm that the same sky I looked into to see the storm clouds raining in my life – were the same clouds I could look into and see the Arms of God wide open for me. In other words, just because the clouds come and it rains in your life – it doesn't mean you will never see the bright sunny sky again. That moment was life changing for me and I pray the words of this book and have been life changing for you.

I lived every single word of this book. Some of the words in this book came forth as tears fell into the keyboard of my laptop. But I was determined to push forth. My prayer for this book was if it could just help one person understand the storm – then the work was fulfilled. The storm clouds are passing – I can see the light of the sun ahead for you. Just look up and you will see it too. And if the storm arrives again – you will know how to hold on until change comes.

I am signing off for now… until next time. Thank you for taking the time to read these words from my heart to yours. I would love to hear your thoughts and feedback about the book. You can reach me via email at stormcloudspass@gmail.com. Be Blessed, Nikki Henderson

ABOUT THE
AUTHOR

Nikki Henderson is a writer and motivational speaker with a message of hope, love, and restoration. Nikki published her first book, entitled "Moments with God: Short Stories for the Soul of a Woman" in 2014. Nikki currently resides in New Jersey with her two sons who are her pride and joy.

Printed in the United States
By Bookmasters